THE LITTLE BOOK OF WISDOM

THE LITTLE BOOK OF
WISDOM

HIS HOLINESS THE
DALAI LAMA

RIDER

LONDON · SYDNEY · AUCKLAND · JOHANNESBURG

This abridged edition published in 2000 by Rider,
an imprint of Ebury Publishing
A Random House Group company

First published in 1997 by Plume,
an imprint of Dutton Signet, Penguin Putnam Inc., USA
Published by Rider in 1998 as
The Dalai Lama's Book of Wisdom.

The Random House Group Limited Reg. No. 954009

Addresses for companies within the Random House
Group can be found at: www.randomhouse.co.uk

Printed and bound in China by Leo Paper Products Ltd.

ISBN 9780712605533

To buy books by your favourite authors and register for
offers visit www.randomhouse.co.uk

ABOUT THE AUTHOR

The immense value of the teachings
of His Holiness the Dalai Lama
have made him, with Mahatma
Gandhi, Mother Teresa and Pope
John Paul II, one of the genuinely
transcendent spiritual figures of our
age. Like these three remarkable
teachers, the Dalai Lama has been
able to reach beyond his Buddhist

devotees to find a universal relevance. Those who revere him do not necessarily adopt Buddhist practices but virtually all derive spiritual and mental enrichment from his insights on daily living, inner peace, compassion, peace and justice.

The Little Book of Wisdom is a timeless collection of advice, comment and sayings from one of the world's most widely known and admired spiritual leaders. It is drawn from a longer work called *The Dalai Lama's Book of Wisdom*, which is also available from Rider, as is *The Dalai Lama's Book of Daily Meditations*.

PART ONE

SPIRITUAL LIFE

LOVE SPRINGS ETERNAL

The foundation of all spiritual
practice is love.

MEDITATE ON THE TRUTH

If we can realise and meditate on
ultimate truth, it will cleanse our
impurities of mind and thus
eradicate the sense of
discrimination.

MEDITATION

Meditation should form the basis
for action.

ULTIMATE TRUTH

In the search for ultimate truth, if it fails to dawn on us, it is we who have not found it. Ultimate truth exists. If we think deeply and reflect carefully, we shall realise that we ourselves have our existence in ultimate truth.

RENUNCIATION

It is said that we should renounce
this life. That doesn't mean that we
should go hungry or not take care
of this lifetime at all, but that we
should reduce our attachment to
affairs that are limited to this
lifetime.

INNER QUIET

If, inside, you possess good qualities, such as compassion or spiritual forgiveness…then external factors will not affect the internal peace of the mind.

KINDNESS BRING
ABOUT PEACE

With kindness, with love and
compassion, with this feeling that
is the essence of brotherhood,
sisterhood, one will have
inner peace.

SPIRITUAL PROGRESS

We must take direct responsibility
for our own spiritual lives and rely
upon nobody and nothing...
If another being were able to save
us, surely he would already have
done so? It is time, therefore, that
we help ourselves.

THE SEEDS OF SPIRITUALITY

The essence of all spiritual life is
your emotion, your attitude
towards others. Once you have
pure and sincere motivation,
all the rest follows.

THE SOURCE OF SPIRITUALITY

The dominant force of our mind is compassion and human affection. Therefore I call these human qualities spirituality.

SPIRITUALITY OUTSIDE OF RELIGION

Without accepting a religion, but simply developing a realisation of the importance of compassion and love, and with more concern and respect for others, a kind of spiritual development is very possible for those persons who are outside of religion.

THE INNER JOURNEY

Purifying the mind is not easy. It takes a lot of time and hard work... You need tremendous willpower and determination right from the start, accepting that there will be many obstacles, and resolving that despite them all you will continue until you have attained your goal.

PRACTISE LOVE

To do so in all situations will take time, but you should not lose courage. If we wish happiness for mankind, love is the only way.

HAPPINESS LIES WITHIN

The very purpose of our life is
happiness: in order to achieve
happier days, happier weeks,
happier years, happier family,
happier human community…we
should pay more attention to inner
development.

CHARACTERISTICS OF THE EVOLVED INDIVIDUAL

We need human qualities such as moral scruples, compassion and humility... These qualities are accessible only through forceful individual development.

FOR THE GOOD OF ALL

Even if only a few individuals try
to create mental peace and
happiness within themselves and
act responsibly and kindheartedly
towards others, they will have a
positive influence in their
community.

FACING PROBLEMS

If, despite external difficulties or
problems, internally one's attitude
is of love, warmth and kindheart-
edness, then problems can be faced
and accepted easily.

HUMILITY

If one assumes a humble attitude,
one's own good qualities will
increase.

RESPECT FOR OTHERS

By developing a sense of respect
for others and a concern for their
welfare, we reduce our own selfish-
ness, which is the source of all
problems, and enhance our sense
of kindness, which is a natural
source of goodness.

ACHIEVING A QUIET MIND

Since even wild animals can
gradually be trained with patience,
the human mind also can gradually
be trained, step by step.

LOVE AND PEACE

Inner tranquillity comes from the
development of love and
compassion.

PART TWO

SELF-DEVELOPMENT

TAKE CONTROL

To make the mind docile, it is
essential for us to discipline and
control it well.

TRAINING THE MIND

Just as a trainer disciplines and calms a wild and wilful steed by subjecting it to skilful and prolonged training, so must the wild, wandering, random activities of body and speech be tamed to make them docile, righteous and skilful.

SELF MASTERY

If someone who easily gets angry
tries to control his or her anger, in
time it can be controlled. The
same is true for a very selfish
person.

THOUGHTS SHAPE EVENTS

All things first originate in the mind. Things and events depend heavily on motivation.

THE IMPORTANCE OF MOTIVATION

The prime mover of every human action is motivation... Our motivation should be simple and sincere. Whether we achieve the goal or not does not matter so long as our motivation is very sincere and we make the attempt.

LEARN FROM YOUR ENEMY

It is the enemy who can try and
teach us to practise the virtues of
compassion and tolerance.
You can learn about the
importance of being patient.
However, the actual practice of
implementing patience comes
when meeting with an enemy.

OVERCOMING DIFFICULTIES

Tolerance is very important. If you have tolerance, you can easily overcome difficulties. If you have little tolerance or are without it, then the smallest thing immediately irritates you.

THE HUMAN COST OF CONSUMER CULTURE

One of the principal factors that hinder us from fully appreciating our interdependence is our undue emphasis on material development. We have become so engrossed in its pursuit that, unknowingly, we have neglected the most basic qualities of compassion, caring and cooperation.

STRIKE A BALANCE

There should be a balance between material and spiritual progress, a balance achieved through the principles based on love and compassion.

THE KEY TO SUCCESS

Determination, with an optimistic
attitude, is the key factor
for success.

INNER VISIONS CREATE OUTER REALITY

If we want a beautiful garden, we must first have a blueprint in the imagination, a vision. Then that idea can be implemented and the external garden can be materialised.

ANALYSE YOUR THOUGHTS...

When we talk about the inner world, there are a lot of different thoughts, or different minds... Those thoughts and actions which ultimately bring happiness, they are positive. Those thoughts and actions which ultimately bring suffering, they are negative.

...THEN FOCUS ON THE POSITIVE

Through mental training you can
increase these positive thoughts
and can reduce negative thoughts.
I can tell you with conviction,
through effort we can change our
mental attitude.

PART THREE

HAPPINESS

THE PURPOSE OF LIFE

Whether we are rich or poor,
educated or uneducated, whatever
our nationality, colour, social
status or ideology may be, the
purpose of our lives is to be happy.

STRIVING AFTER WORLDLY SUCCESS

If striving thus were really productive of permanent happiness, then among the many people in this world endowed with power, wealth and friendship, there would surely be some blessed with a large measure of real and lasting happiness.

HAPPINESS CAN'T BE BOUGHT

Mental peace cannot be injected by any doctor; no market can sell mental peace or happiness.

PEACE LIES WITHIN

We are trying to get peace
or happiness from outside, from
money or power. But real peace,
tranquillity, should come from
within.

THE KEY TO FULFILMENT

Unless our minds are stable and
calm, no matter how comfortable
our physical condition may be,
they will give us no pleasure.
Therefore, the key to a happy life,
now and in the future, is to
develop a happy mind.

AS YOU SOW, SO YOU REAP

Happiness comes from kindness.
Happiness cannot come from
hatred or anger.

THE RIPPLE EFFECT

If an individual human being
eventually becomes a nice, calm,
peaceful person, then it
automatically brings some kind of
positive atmosphere, and you have
a happy family.

PART FOUR

LOVE & COMPASSION

LOVE IS THE CENTRE OF HUMAN LIFE

Love and compassion…are the
ultimate source of human
happiness, and our need for them
lies at the very core of our being.

A GOOD HEART

A good mind, a good heart, warm
feelings – these are the most
important things.

REAL LOVE

Real love is not based on attachment.

LOVE DOES NOT DISCRIMINATE

The kind of love we advocate is the love you can have even for someone who has done harm to you. This kind of love is to be extended to all living beings, and it can be extended to all living beings.

LOVE IS HARD

Compassion and love are precious things in life. They are not complicated. They are simple, but difficult to practise.

LOVE YOUR ENEMY

If you have love and compassion
toward all sentient beings,
particularly toward your enemy,
that is true love and compassion.

THE GREATNESS OF MATERNAL LOVE

The feeling of a mother for her child is a classic example of love. For the safety, protection and welfare of her children, a mother is ready to sacrifice her very life.

LOVE ONE ANOTHER

Human beings are social creatures,
and a concern for each other is the
very basis of our life together.

LOVE'S CONSOLATION

Love…consoles when one is helpless and distressed, and it consoles when one is old and lonely. It is a dynamic force that we should develop and use, but often tend to neglect, particularly in our prime years, when we experience a false sense of security.

DO AS YOU WOULD BE DONE BY

Since at the beginning and end of our lives we are so dependent on others' kindness, how can it be that in the middle we neglect kindness towards others.

THE MORE YOU GIVE, THE MORE YOU RECEIVE

The more we care for the happiness of others, the greater is our own sense of well-being.

LOVE CONQUERS ALL

Cultivating a close, warmhearted feeling for others automatically puts the mind at ease and opens our inner door. It helps remove whatever fears or insecurities we may have and gives us the strength to cope with any obstacles we encounter. It is the principal source of success in life.

LOVE IS ALWAYS APPROPRIATE

Love and kindness are always appropriate. Whether or not you believe in rebirth, you will need love in this life. If we have love, there is hope to have real families, real brotherhood, real equanimity, real peace.

EVERY ONE OF US HAS THE CAPACITY FOR KINDNESS

The development of a kind heart, or feeling of closeness for all human beings, does not involve any of the kind of religiosity we normally associate with it... It is for everyone, irrespective of race, religion or any political affiliation.

THE WAY FORWARD

As a human being, kindness, a warm heart, is very important… If you have this basic quality of kindness or good heart, then all other things, education, ability, will go in the right direction.

PUT OTHERS FIRST

Our doings and thinkings must
be motivated by compassion for
others. The way to acquire that
kind of outlook is to accept the
simple fact that whatever we desire
is also desired by others.

GENUINE COMPASSION

Genuine compassion is unbiased,
should be unbiased.

COMPASSION IS BORN OF RESPECT

Genuine compassion must be acting on the basis of respect, and the realisation or recognition that others also, just like myself, have the right to be happy.

COMPASSION REACHES OUT TO ALL

Compassion compels us to reach out to all living beings, including our so-called enemies, those people who upset or hurt us. Irrespective of what they do to you, if you remember that all beings like you are only trying to be happy, you will find it much easier to develop compassion towards them.

COMPASSION IS A SIGN OF INNER STRENGTH

Compassion is, by nature, peaceful
and gentle, but it is also very
powerful.

FINDING YOUR WAY

Each of us in our own way can try to spread compassion into people's hearts.

COMPASSION IS RESPONSIBLE

To experience genuine compassion is to develop a feeling of closeness to others combined with a sense of responsibility for their welfare.

COMPASSION IS
COMMITTED

True compassion is not just an
emotional response but a firm
commitment founded on reason.

COMPASSION IS CONSTANT

A truly compassionate attitude
towards others does not change,
even if they behave negatively.

PART FIVE

THE INNER ENEMIES

THE ENEMY IN YOUR HEART

There is one enemy who is always an enemy, with whom you should never compromise; that is the enemy inside your heart. You cannot change all these bad thoughts into your friend, but you have to confront and control them.

THE ROOT OF ALL PROBLEMS

Anger, attachment, jealousy, hatred…these are the real enemy.

NEGATIVITY IS NEVER THE SOLUTION

Anger, jealousy, impatience and hatred are the real troublemakers; with them problems cannot be solved. Though one may have temporary success, ultimately one's hatred or anger will create further difficulties.

NO GOOD EVER CAME OF ANGER

Anger may seem to offer an energetic way of getting things done, but such a perception of the world is misguided. The only certainty about anger and hatred is that they are destructive.

TWO KINDS OF ANGER

Anger I think can be of two types:
hatred with ill-feeling is one while
another anger – with compassion
as the basis of concern – may be
positive.

KEEP ANGER IN CHECK

Usually people consider that anger
is part of the mind, and that it is
better to show it, to let it come. I
think that's the wrong
conception... Resentment because
of grievances may be let out,
because then it is finished...
Constant anger – that,
I think, it is better to check.

TWO WRONGS DON'T MAKE A RIGHT

Hatred cannot be overcome by
hatred... Hatred will only generate
more problems.

FEAR

Fear arises when we view everyone
else with suspicion.

THE PATH TO SELF-DESTRUCTION

If we live our lives continually motivated by anger and hatred, even our physical health deteriorates.

VIOLENCE IS
SELF-PERPETUATING

If you succeed through violence at
the expense of others' rights and
welfare, you have not solved the
problem, but only created the
seeds for another.

SELF-IMPORTANCE

Tolerance and patience with courage are not signs of failure but signs of victory... Actually, if you are too important, that's a real failure.

PART SIX

MORAL VALUES

CAUSE AND EFFECT

One's own actions create one's life
situation.

THE POWER OF LOVE

A good heart is both important and
effective in daily life.

REAPING THE BENEFITS

The reason why we seek to behave
in a good manner is that it's from
good behaviour that good fruits are
derived.

BUILDING A BETTER LIFE

One wants happiness and doesn't want suffering, and on the basis of that, one enters into good actions and avoids bad actions.

GUIDING PRINCIPLES

Be guided by realism, moderation,
and patience.

WORK FOR THE WELFARE OF ALL

With a pure heart, you can carry on any work…and your profession becomes a real instrument to help the human community.

PURITY OF INTENTION

Once you have pure and sincere
motivation, all the rest follows.
You can develop this right attitude
towards others on the basis of
kindness, love and respect, and on
the clear realisation of the oneness
of all human beings.

CARING FOR OTHERS

Most of the good or beneficial
effects that come about in the
world are based on an attitude of
cherishing others. The opposite is
also true.

GIVE AND TAKE

By showing concern for other
people's welfare, sharing other
people's suffering, and helping
other people, ultimately one will
benefit. If one thinks only of
oneself and forgets about others,
ultimately one will lose.

LOOK AHEAD

It is more important to look forward to the future than dwell in the past.

THE PARADOX OF SELF-INTEREST

If we adopt a self-centred approach to life by which we attempt to use others for our own self-interest, we might be able to gain temporary benefit, but in the long run we will not succeed in achieving even our personal happiness.

OPTIMISM ACHIEVES GREATNESS

An optimistic attitude is the key factor for success. Right from the beginning, if you hold a pessimistic attitude even small things may not be achieved.

SIGNS OF SUCCESS

In your daily life, as you learn
more patience, more tolerance with
wisdom and courage, you will see
it is the true source of success.

GOOD COMMUNICATIONS

Compassion…opens an inner door,
and once through the door we can
communicate with other fellow
human beings and other sentient
beings.

TEACH BY EXAMPLE

Before teaching others, before
changing others, we ourselves must
change. We must be honest,
sincere, kind-hearted.

DO AS YOU WOULD BE DONE BY

We should share the sufferings of our fellow human beings and practise compassion and tolerance, not only towards our loved ones but towards our enemies.

WORK FOR THE WELFARE OF OTHERS

Our daily thoughts and actions should be directed towards the benefit of others.

PRACTISE WHAT YOU PREACH

We should engage in the same high standards of integrity and sacrifice that we ask of others.

DON'T BE SEDUCED BY WORLDLY VALUES

Materialism does not foster the growth of morals, compassion and humility.

TAKE RESPONSIBILITY FOR THOSE IN NEED

It is the nature of human beings to yearn for freedom, equality and dignity. If we accept that others have a right to peace and happiness equal to our own, do we not have a responsibility to help those in need?

TAKE ACTION

No one can afford to assume that someone else will solve our problems. Every individual has a responsibility to help guide our human family in the right direction. Good wishes are not sufficient.

THE MORAL CODE

Irrespective of whether we are a believer or an agnostic, whether we believe in God or karma, moral ethics is a code which everyone is able to pursue.

THE MORAL PERSPECTIVE

To pursue growth properly, we
need to renew our commitment to
human values in many fields.
Political life, of course, requires an
ethical foundation, but science and
religion as well should be pursued
from a moral basis.

PART SEVEN

FAMILY & FRIENDS

TRUE FRIENDSHIP

The proper way to create friends is through a warm heart and not simple money or power. Friends of power and friends of money are something different. These are not friends.

MAKING FRIENDS

If we have a kind and loving heart
we will win more friends.

BE FRIENDLY

Friends are very important, as are
a friendly manner and a genuine
smile.

SMILE FROM THE HEART

A genuine smile must come from
the face of compassion.

MUTUAL INTEREST

If you want friends and a friendly atmosphere, you must create the basis for them. Whether the other's response will be positive or not, first you must create some kind of common ground.

CREATE A PEACEFUL ENVIRONMENT

If in a small family, even without children, the members have a warm heart to each other, a peaceful atmosphere will be created. However, if one of the persons feels angry, immediately the atmosphere in the house becomes tense.

CHERISH ONE ANOTHER

If we cherish others, then both
others and ourselves, both deeply
and superficially, will be happy...
When we cherish ourselves more
than others...we produce various
types of suffering, both for
ourselves and for those around us.

LIVING IN HARMONY

Peaceful living is about trusting
those on whom we depend and
caring for those who depend on us.

BE FORGIVING

When we are able to recognise and
forgive ignorant actions of the
past, we gain the strength to solve
the problems of the past
constructively.

COMPASSION BUILDS TRUST

It is compassion that creates
the sense of trust that allows us to
open up to others and reveal our
problems, doubts and
uncertainties.

HOW CHILDREN THRIVE

Children whose homes have love
and affection are better, healthier,
normal and sturdy. Where children
lack human affection and love,
physical development is sometimes
difficult, as is study.

CHILDHOOD DEPRIVATION

Children who had difficulties at an early age, growing under a lack of human love and affection, will find it difficult to show other humans love and compassion. And that's a great tragedy, a great tragedy.

PART EIGHT

BUDDHISM

LOVE AND COMPASSION

The essence of Buddhism is
kindness, compassion. This is the
essence of every religion.

ALL ARE EQUAL

Central to the Buddha's teaching is seeing the equality among humanity and the importance of equality of all sentient beings. Whether you are a Buddhist or not, this is something important to know and understand.

AVOID INJURY TO OTHERS

Destruction or injury to life is strictly forbidden. Harming or destroying any being from the highest to the lowest, from a human to the tiniest insect, must at all costs be avoided.

ACTIONS SPEAK LOUDER THAN WORDS

Merely to call oneself a Buddhist
is of little value.

THE BUDDHA'S TEACHINGS

The Buddha himself taught different things according to the place, the occasion and the situation of those who were listening to him.

REAL CHANGE TAKES PLACE ON THE INSIDE

If you have adopted Buddhism you should not consider yourself a 'great Buddhist' and immediately start to do everything differently. A Tibetan proverb states, 'Change your mind but leave your appearance as usual.'

ABSOLUTE TRUTH

From the viewpoint of absolute truth, what we feel and experience in our ordinary daily life is all delusion.

THE HUMAN CONDITION

All other beings are just like us in
that they want happiness and
dislike suffering.

THE UNIVERSALITY OF SUFFERING

Every single one of us – be he a ruler or warrior, be he rich, middle-class, or poor – is subject to all sorts of physical and mental suffering, especially torments of the mind.

THE ULTIMATE DELUSION

Of all the various delusions, the sense of discrimination between oneself and others is the worst form, as it creates nothing but unpleasantness for both sides.

PART NINE

RELIGION

MANY WAYS, ONE TRUTH

Despite the differences in the
names and forms used by the
various religions, the ultimate truth
to which they point is the same.

TOLERANCE

Practitioners of different faiths should realise that each religious tradition has immense intrinsic value as a means for providing mental and spiritual health.

A GOOD HEART

Religion is not something outside,
but in our hearts. The essence of
any religion is a good heart.

THE VEHICLES OF TRUTH

No one religion is appropriate for all types of people. Just as Buddhism is not best for everyone, Christianity is not appropriate for all types of disposition.

FOOD FOR THOUGHT

Religion is a food for the mind,
and as we all have different tastes,
we must take that which is most
suitable for us.

THE ROLE OF RELIGION

Western civilisations these days
place great importance on filling
the human brain with knowledge,
but no one seems to care about
filling the human heart with
compassion. This is what the real
role of religion is.

PRACTICE IS MORE IMPORTANT THAN THEORY

It is much more beneficial to try to implement daily the shared precepts for goodness taught by all religions rather than to argue about minor differences in approach.

LIVE BY YOUR BELIEFS

All major religions are basically
the same in that they emphasise
peace of mind and kindness, but it
is very important to practise this in
our daily lives, not just in a church
or temple.

THE GOAL OF RELIGION

The purpose of religion is not to
build beautiful churches or
temples, but to cultivate positive
human qualities, such as tolerance,
generosity and love.

THE COMMONALITY OF ALL RELIGIONS

Every religion of the world has similar ideals of love, the same goal of benefiting humanity through spiritual practice, and the same effect of making its followers into better human beings... Each, in its own way, teaches a path leading to a spiritual state that is peaceful, disciplined, ethical and wise.

PURITY OF HEART

If the motivation is sincere, then every human action can be positive – including political initiatives. If our motivation is not adequate, not pure, even religion becomes smeared.

TAKING THE NAME OF RELIGION IN VAIN

Sometimes in the name of religion people cause more quarrels than they solve.

PART TEN

WORLD PEACE

THE BASIS FOR WORLD PEACE

Genuine peace, genuine lasting world peace, can be achieved only through inner peace.

UNIVERSAL RESPONSIBILITY

Universal responsibility is the key to human survival. It is the best foundation for world peace.

THE EXTERNAL WORLD REFLECTS OUR INNER REALITIES

The well-being of society…
depends upon the internal attitude
of the people who compose it.

INGREDIENTS FOR PEACE

Through kindness…through
mutual understanding and through
mutual respect we will get peace,
we will get happiness, and we will
get genuine satisfaction.

PRACTISE KINDNESS

It is very difficult to achieve peace and harmony through competition and hatred, so the practice of kindness is very, very important and very, very valuable in human society.

LOVE AND COMPASSION

Love and compassion are the moral
fabric of world peace.

PART ELEVEN

GLOBAL ISSUES

UNNECESSARY SUFFERING

Humans must face death, old age and disease as well as natural disasters, such as hurricanes, that are beyond our control... But these sufferings are quite sufficient for us. Why should we create other problems due to our own ideology, just different ways of thinking?

GLOBAL CHANGE BEGINS
WITH INDIVIDUAL ACTION

For any change, and movement
in the human community, the
initiative must come from
individuals.

UNIVERSAL BENEFITS

When we are motivated by wisdom
and compassion, the results of our
actions benefit everyone, not just
our individual selves or some
immediate convenience.

MUTUAL INTERESTS

The more we become interdependent, the more it is in our interest to ensure the well-being of others.

CONCERN FOR OTHERS

When we do not know someone or do not feel connected to an individual or group, we tend to overlook their needs. Yet the development of human society requires that people help each other.

ETHICS IN PUBLIC LIFE

It is an absurd assumption that
religion and morality have no place
in politics.

'WE' AND 'THEY'

The whole world is becoming
smaller and smaller. The concept
of 'we' and 'they' is gone,
out of date.

PART TWELVE

DEATH & LIBERATION

ETERNAL LIFE

At the moment we are blessed with human life and with all the possibilities that this implies. When we die nothing can be taken with us but the seeds of our life's work and our spiritual knowledge.

THE IMPERMANENCE OF MIND

Since experience and knowledge are impermanent and subject to disintegration, the mind of which they are functions is not something that remains constant and eternal.

TIME IS PRECIOUS:
USE IT WELL

If we use this human brain for
something of little import, that is
very sad. If we spend our time just
concerned with the affairs of this
lifetime up to the point of death,
that is very sad and weak.

ULTIMATE DEATH

In ultimate death, if I search for
myself I will not find it, and if you
search for yourselves you will not
find them.